WHEN Doves CRAFT

10 Projects Inspired by the Artist

INSIGHT EDITIONS

San Rafael • Los Angeles • London

Contents

PURPLE *Crane*

I only want to see you laughing
with your purple crane

26

Raspberry CROCHET

Not the kind you find in
a second-hand store

32

YOU GOT THE *Scrapbook*

A cut-out-and-keep
Prince to add to your fan album

38

NO PARTICULAR *Sign*

Create a hand-painted sign for your home

44

Snow IN APRIL

Try your hand at seasonal papercraft

50

YOUR EXTRA TIME AND YOUR *Stitch*

Cross-stitch your favorite lyrics

56

Macrame YOUR MAMA HAPPY

With this sensational wall hanging

Whittle RED CROCHET HOOK

Woodwork a love that's gonna last

Introduction

There is no denying that Prince was a musical genius. We have all heard his songs played on the radio and watched his music videos, and some of us were even lucky enough to see him performing on stage. He wrote music and lyrics as well as played numerous instruments—and, of course, sang vocals. But his creativity was not limited to the musical arena. From his sanctuary at Paisley Park, Prince explored design and color, decorating the space with everything from plush purple velvet couches, to a "galaxy room" to practice meditation. In the same way that Prince blended musical styles, he also combined design, pattern, and color, creating his own signature look that was as unique and kooky as he was. As a true individual, we can learn a lot from Prince about doing our own thing and creating our own path in life.

In this book, we have showcased projects that use a range of craft materials and skills to help you be creative, experiment, and try new things. We have paid homage to Prince not only as a musical icon, but also as an icon of creativity and self-expression. Although we cannot all be musical geniuses like he was, through crafting we can at least attempt to bring a touch of his flair and style into our lives.

Recently, there has been a lot of talk around the mental and physical benefits of exploring creativity through crafting objects by hand. There is something so intrinsically satisfying about making something with your hands. There is a sense of accomplishment when you finish a project and can proudly say "I made that," and you can become so totally absorbed in a task that you do not realize how much time has passed. It's this feeling of absorption and complete focus on the task at hand that draws so many people to creative activities, and to lead intensely creative lives like Prince did. In this book, we have combined our love of crafts with our deep love of Prince to create ten fun projects that we hope will encourage your creativity.

Sonia & Zoe, London Craft Club

Projects

Prince FINGER PUPPET

The spirit of Prince at your fingertips

Prince changed our lives back in 1984. Totally sexy and wildly experimental, *Purple Rain* the album, tour, and movie were like nothing we'd seen before. Here was the story of Prince's life—and it rocked!

From that moment on, everyone knew Prince and, what's more, they knew what he looked like. He used the power of frills, smoke, and purple to catch our attention, although sometimes his outré style slightly overshadowed his musicianship. But there's no denying his creative and technical virtuosity, so we've made sure that our Prince Finger Puppet has his guitar. See if you can capture the way he held it when you sew it in place. Take a little time to embellish it with anything extra you think he'd have enjoyed, adding lace or organza to really ramp up the ruffles.

YOU WILL NEED:

- Black, purple, and skin-tone felt (one small sheet of each)
- Pair of scissors
- Thread in black, purple, white and skin tone
- Stiff white fabric (for his shirt)
- Sewing needle
- Straight pins
- Pattern template printed on paper (see page 79)

1 Cut out the colored shapes from the patterns (see page 79) and pin them to the pieces of felt. Don't forget to cut out two guitars. Make sure the straight pins don't stick out over the edge of the paper or you'll ruin your scissors when you cut out the shapes.

2 Using the scissors, cut out the shapes from the felt and your white shirt fabric. Sharp fabric scissors make this a lot easier, but you can do it with any pair of scissors you have.

3 Lay the two jacket sides onto Prince's body, and tuck the white shirt parts under the edges of the collar and the sleeves. Pin it all together and sew it in place using purple thread (we've used a basic running stitch here). Don't forget to add frilly cuffs to both the front and back.

4   Pin the back of Prince's jacket on and use purple thread to sew the front and back together along the sides of his body and arms. We've used a whipstitch here, but you can use a blanket stitch if you prefer.

5   Pin the front and back of Prince's hair in position and use black thread to sew the pieces together in the same way you did for the jacket. Be respectful—Prince hated strangers touching his hair.

6   Put the two pieces of guitar together and sew all the way around it with black thread. You can stuff pieces of cotton ball or lentils inside the guitar to make it firm, if you prefer.

7 Cut out your templates for Prince's neckpiece out of the white fabric and layer them up, pinning and then stitching into place at the top with white thread.

Did you know?

The costume designers on *Purple Rain*, Louis Wells and Marie France, were inspired by seventeenth-century clothes to create his frothy, ruffled shirt.

8 Use black thread to sew on a pair of eyes and skin-tone thread to sew his hands in place on the guitar. We used a French knot for his eyes, but just a few little stitches will do the job, too.

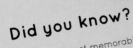
I WOULD *Dye* FOR YOU

Try the craft formerly known as batik

Prince was off the wall. We all know this and love him for it. But really, attaching your name to a symbol is true rock-star behavior. The final version, designed by Mitch Monson and Lizz Luce, had a hand-drawn quality at Prince's insistence. He called it the "Love Symbol," and from 1993 to 2000 he refused to be known by any of his previous titles. To the world, he became "The Artist Formerly Known as Prince."

The Love Symbol was a headache for the press and his record label Warner Bros. alike, and in large part it was a product of the battle with the record label over the copyright of Prince's name. But there was more to it. Typically for Prince, it was a statement about the fluidity of gender and sexuality, and it remains a symbol of acceptance, creativity, and love. Make this batik scarf embellished with decorative symbols of your own and celebrate Prince's individuality.

YOU WILL NEED:

- Plain white cotton scarf (lightweight)
- ¼ cup (50 g) beeswax pellets
- Small saucepan
- Small artist's paintbrush
- Plastic container
- Purple cold dye (hot dye will not work)
- Rubber gloves
- Paper towels
- An iron
- Symbol template printed on paper (see page 81)

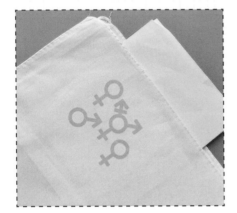

1 Lay your cotton scarf over your symbol template; you should be able to see it through the cotton, like tracing paper. Alternatively, create your own, freehand decorative symbol template.

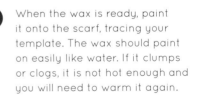

2 Slowly heat up the wax in a small saucepan on the stove until it has completely melted and is as runny and clear as water. If it starts to bubble, spit, or smoke, remove it from the heat immediately. Never leave the wax on the stove unattended and always be careful when handling it.

3 When the wax is ready, paint it onto the scarf, tracing your template. The wax should paint on easily like water. If it clumps or clogs, it is not hot enough and you will need to warm it again.

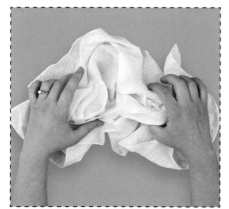

4 Some of the wax will seep through the headscarf and onto the paper below. Peel the headscarf off the paper, move it to a new position, and paint on another symbol in wax. You will need to keep reheating the wax. If your brush is clogged with wax, just hold the bristles in the hot wax. Watch it melt away and the brush will be soft again.

5 When you have finished painting on the wax, let it cool and harden. You can crunch it up a little to get the crackled batik effect, but don't let the wax crack off completely.

6 Wearing rubber gloves, mix the dye in the plastic container, following the package instructions. Carefully lower in the scarf and let it soak for 20 minutes.

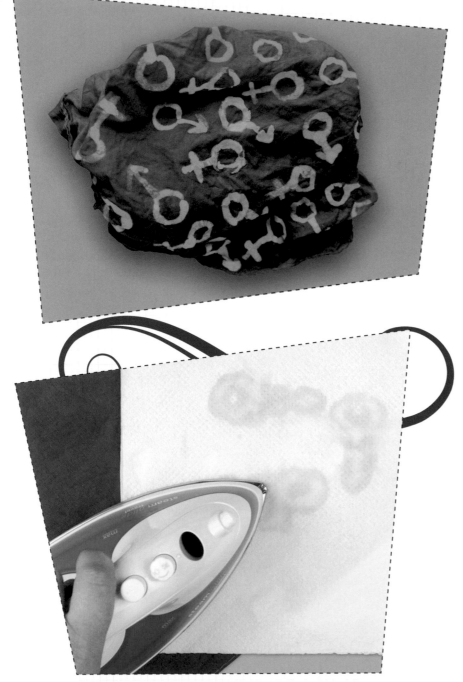

7 Still wearing the gloves, remove the scarf from the container and rinse it under cold running water. Be careful not to drip the dye, because it can stain clothes and surfaces. When the water runs clear, let the scarf dry.

8 When it's dry, place two sheets of paper towel under the scarf and two on top. Iron the scarf through the paper towels, and watch the wax soak into the towel. Keep ironing until no more wax comes off. The fabric will be stiff from the wax but, if you want, you can wash it at a warm temperature and it will soften up.

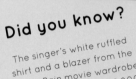

PURPLE *Crane*

YOU WILL NEED:

- Square pieces of paper (any size and color—but preferably purple)
- Purple water-based or acrylic paint
- Artist's paintbrush
- Needle
- Thread
- Glue gun
- Wooden embroidery hoop

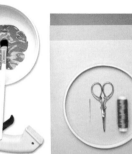

I just want to see you laughing with your purple crane

Purple has long been known as the color of royalty, but no royal has ever done the color justice in the same way as Prince.

Back in 1984, when the *Purple Rain* album, movie, and single were released, his ownership of the color was comprehensively confirmed. He chose the color for good reason. Throughout history, purple has been an emblem of royalty, mainly because it was such an expensive dye to make. Nowadays, it's associated with indulgence, luxury, mystery, and sensuality—so, of course, it would be Prince's color.

In this next craft, you can make it rain purple cranes. Go for a selection of purple papers and really explore the hue—the more cranes you make, the better.

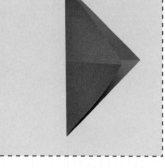

1 Place a square piece of paper on a surface. You can use any size square, but at first it's easier to learn with a larger square.

2 Fold the paper in half diagonally, then open it up and fold diagonally the other way. You should have an X-shape fold across your paper.

3 Flip the paper over so you're working on the opposite side. Fold in half horizontally and open up again, then fold in half vertically to create creases in an eight-point star shape.

5 Turn your square 45 degrees so that it is a diamond. Make sure the open part of the folds are at the bottom.

4 Rotate the paper 45 degrees so that it is a diamond, then bring the left and right points of the diamond together. At the same time, the top and bottom points should automatically fold inward and come together. This forms an origami "square base."

6 Bring the bottom left and right edges of the top two layers of paper in toward the fold in the center, which runs from the top to the bottom of the diamond.

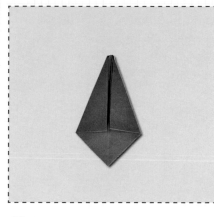

7 Repeat on the other side, so you end up with a kite shape.

8 Unfold the side you just folded in. At the bottom of the kite, take the top layer of paper and pull it up and back, drawing the sides in as you do so. You'll need to reverse some the creases you have made.

9 Turn the paper over and repeat on the other side. This will give you two wings.

10 Fold the bottom left edge into the crease in the center.

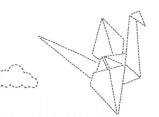

 Repeat on the right, then flip the paper over and repeat on the other side.

 Fold the bottom left prong back and forth to create a crease. Reverse the crease along the length of the prong, and fold inward and upward to create the crane's tail.

 Repeat on the other side to create the neck.

 Halfway down the neck, create a reverse fold for the head.

Fold the two side sections down to create wings. If you want, paint on details, such as eyes or a beak.

16 Using sewing thread and a needle, thread through the center of your crane from bottom to top. Attach as many cranes as you want onto each piece of thread. Add a tiny drop of glue from a glue gun where the thread comes out of each crane to stop it from sliding to the bottom of the thread.

17 Take the inner circle of a wooden embroidery hoop and paint it purple. To create your mobile, hang as many lengths of cranes as you want from the hoop, and it is ready to be displayed.

Video:

Raspberry CROCHET

- 1/9 (5.5 mm/5) crochet hook
- Aran-weight yarn (we used Stylecraft Special Aran in Raspberry)
- Pair of scissors

No second-hand beret to be found? Crochet your own!

Arguably Prince's most perfect pop song, "Raspberry Beret" was released in 1985 on *Around the World in a Day*. It was an instant worldwide hit, and it remains a pop anthem and radio favorite nearly thirty years on.

In Prince's typical inimitable style, the girl in the beret who steals his heart is sturdy and not too bright, but she's rebellious nonetheless. If you've been scouring the second-hand stores for a raspberry beret but come up empty handed, you can crochet one of your own. According to Prince, when the weather is warm, this is all you'll need to wear anyway.

Creating this slouchy hat will require basic knowledge on how to crochet, but if you're new to crocheting, no problem! Use the QR code above, which will lead you to instructional videos on the London Craft Club website. Remember, however, the video uses British terms—a U.K. treble crochet is a U.S. double crochet. The steps here, of course, follow U.S. terms.

The first ch3 of each round counts as a dc.
At the end of each round sl st to join, and then sl st
around until you reach the first chain space.

1 Ch and join with sl st to first ch to form a ring.

2 Ch3 (counts as first dc), 1dc into ring. *Ch1, 2dc* five times. Ch1 and sl st to join.

3 Work into chain space between the pairs of dc. Ch3, dc, ch1, 2dc into first space. *2dc, ch1, 2dc* into each of the other spaces.

4 Ch3, 2dc into first space. *Ch1, 3dc* in each space.

5 Repeat step 4.

6 Repeat step 4.

7 Ch3, dc, ch1, 2dc into first space. *2dc, ch1, 2dc* in each space.

 8 Ch3, 2dc into first space. *Ch1, 3dc* in each space.

 9 Repeat step 8.

 **10** Ch3, 2dc into first space. *In next space, ch1, 3dc, ch1, then into following space 3dc, ch1, 3dc.* Repeat to the end.

 **11** Ch3, 2dc into first space. *Ch1, 3dc* in each space.

12 Repeat round 11.

13 Repeat round 11.

 14 Ch3, 2dc into first space. *Ch1, 3dc* into each of the next two spaces, then ch1, 3dc, ch1, 3dc into following space. Repeat to the end.

 15 Ch3, 2dc into first space. *Ch1, 3dc* in each space.

 16 Ch2. *Hdc in the next two stitches, hdc dec across the next two stitches.* Repeat to the end.

17 Repeat round 16.

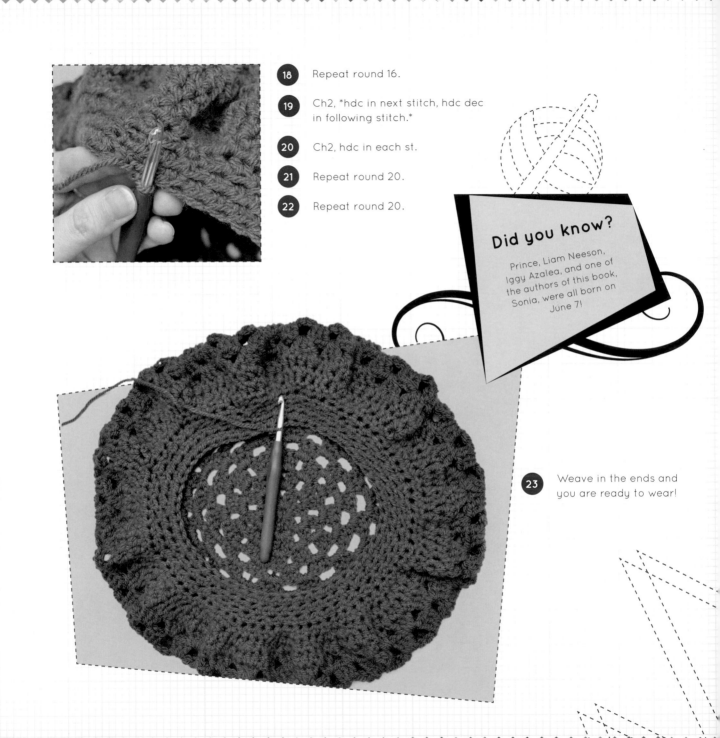

18 Repeat round 16.

19 Ch2, *hdc in next stitch, hdc dec in following stitch.*

20 Ch2, hdc in each st.

21 Repeat round 20.

22 Repeat round 20.

Did you know?

Prince, Liam Neeson, Iggy Azalea, and one of the authors of this book, Sonia, were all born on June 7!

23 Weave in the ends and you are ready to wear!

YOU GOT THE *Scrapbook*

A cut-out-and-keep paper Prince

Prince really could do everything, so where do we start when putting together a scrapbook of his musical talents?

He was a prolific writer, composer, producer, singer, and musician, and he famously played twenty-seven instruments. However, Prince was the most prodigiously skilled at playing the guitar. Search any list of the best guitar solos and you'll be sure to find a Prince performance in there.

Perhaps the most emotionally charged of his performances was that of the Beatles' hit "While My Guitar Gently Weeps" at the induction of George Harrison into the Rock & Roll Hall of Fame. Prince took the final solo and made it sublimely his own, alongside George's son Dhani and Tom Petty.

Our scrapbook just wouldn't be complete without our own paper tribute to Prince and his incredible shredding cred.

YOU WILL NEED:

- Colored card stock (we used bright blue, pale blue, white, black, cream, and brown, but you can use other colors, if you want)
- Self-healing cutting mat
- Craft knife with blade
- Masking tape
- Glue stick or double-sided tape
- Prince template printed on paper (see page 83)

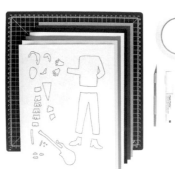

1. Start by checking your template, so you know how many of each piece you will be cutting and which color they should be cut from, making a note of your color choices. You don't want to accidentally give Prince blue hands!

2. Tape down your first sheet of colored card stock onto your self-healing cutting mat, using masking tape, then tape the template sheet on top.

 Using your craft knife, cut out the pieces you've decided should be that color (for example, cut the pieces labeled "white" from the white card stock). You will cut through both the template sheet and the card stock underneath.

For advice about cutting, see the Top Tips box in the Snow in April project.

 Simply repeat the process with the other sheets of colored card stock until you have cut out all the pieces on the template sheet.

5 Once you've finished cutting all your pieces, arrange them carefully using the project photo as a guide to how they should fit together. Start with the largest pieces, then layer the smaller pieces on top.

6 Secure each piece in place with a dab of glue or a piece of double-sided tape until your Prince is completely formed. This is just the start of your scrapbooking journey! Fill the rest of your book with sketches, stickers, photos, and notes. You can even repeat this project using different colors of card stock to create a variety of outfits for your paper Prince.

NO PARTICULAR *Sign*

YOU WILL NEED:

- Piece of wood (we used a wooden cutting board that we cut to size)
- Sandpaper
- Design template printed on paper (see page 85)
- Carbon paper
- Masking tape
- Pencil
- Acrylic paints in purple and white
- Paintbrush

Signpost your Prince fandom

If you're in a band or are an artist, how do you signpost your admiration for another artist's work? By covering it, of course.

However, Prince adamantly defended the rights of artists to control the use of their creative output, fighting to keep his own work off streaming services and often refusing permission for covers, most famously denying the Foo Fighters' request to cover "Darling Nikki." He allegedly said, "When I want to hear new music, I go make some."

However, in a mysterious gesture not understood by anyone, he covered the Foo Fighters' song "Have It All" at his legendary 2007 Super Bowl appearance. The story goes that the band preferred the Purple One's rendition.

Make sure your piece of wood is clean and smooth, ready to paint on. If there are any rough patches, you can use a piece of sandpaper to smooth them out.

 Lay a piece of carbon paper on the wood, then lay your template on top. Secure them in place with masking tape.

3 To transfer the design onto your piece of wood, trace over its outlines with the pencil. Be careful not to press too hard.

4 Remove the carbon paper and template, and check to make sure the design has transferred onto the wood properly. If there are any gaps or faint areas, just go over them lightly with the pencil.

Did you know?

Prince was a huge Joni Mitchell fan. The singer saw him in the front row at one of her concerts, and he regularly sent her fan letters. He even covered her song "A Case of You."

5 Choose your first color of paint and decide which areas you will paint that color. If it helps, you can mark lightly with pencil, to remember which elements you'd like in which color.

We recommend starting with the lighter colors, and finishing with the darker colors.

6 Begin painting, being careful to follow the outlines carefully and apply an even layer of paint. Repeat with each color of paint, letter each color dry before applying the next, until the entire design has been painted. Let dry before finding an appropriate place to display your sign!

Snow IN APRIL

YOU WILL NEED:

- Wooden embroidery hoop
- White acrylic paint
- Paintbrush
- Colored card stock (we used different shades of blue)
- Self-healing cutting mat
- Masking tape
- 2–3 copies of the snowflake template printed on paper (see page 87)
- Scissors
- Craft knife with blade
- Glue gun
- Ribbon

This paper snowflake wreath is a delicate memento

It is said that the song "Sometimes It Snows in April" was recorded exactly thirty-one years to the day before Prince himself died.

A tragic tale in itself, the song tells the story of the death of Prince's character Christopher Tracy in his self-directed movie *Under the Cherry Moon*, and many of Prince's fans now view it as the ultimate eulogy to the singer.

The song has been covered by the American artist D'Angelo, UK band the Futureheads, Australian singer-songwriter Gotye, and many others. It may never have been released as a single, but on his death it charted in many countries around the world.

So take a little time to remember one of Prince's most beautiful songs as you carefully cut this paper snowflake wreath. We've tried to keep it plain and simple, just like the song, and we leave it to you to find the love in creating and assembling it.

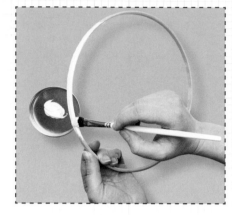

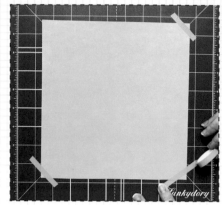

1 Start by taking apart your embroidery hoop and painting the inner hoop white all over. Let dry while you move on to the next steps of the project.

2 Tape your first sheet of colored card stock onto your self-healing cutting mat, using masking tape.

3 Choose two or three snowflakes to cut out of your first color of card stock, and roughly cut these away from the rest of the template.

4 Tape your first templates over the card stock—you will be cutting through both the template and the card stock at the same time. Press just hard enough that your knife cuts through both the materials. It may take a couple of attempts to get the amount of pressure right.

5 Once you've cut out the snowflakes you want from the first color, repeat with your other colors of card stock until you have 8–12 snowflakes.

6 Arrange your snowflakes on your painted embroidery hoop, mixing up the colors and sizes of snowflakes until you're happy with how they are placed.

When cutting a corner, always start from the corner and cut away from it, cause this will help the blade to cut right into the corner without going too far.

Curves can be difficult to cut, so take your time. Don't try to cut the whole thing in one attempt, and keep turning your work as you cut.

Hold your craft knife in the same way you hold a pen, making sure the blade at about a 45-degree angle to the paper you are cutting.

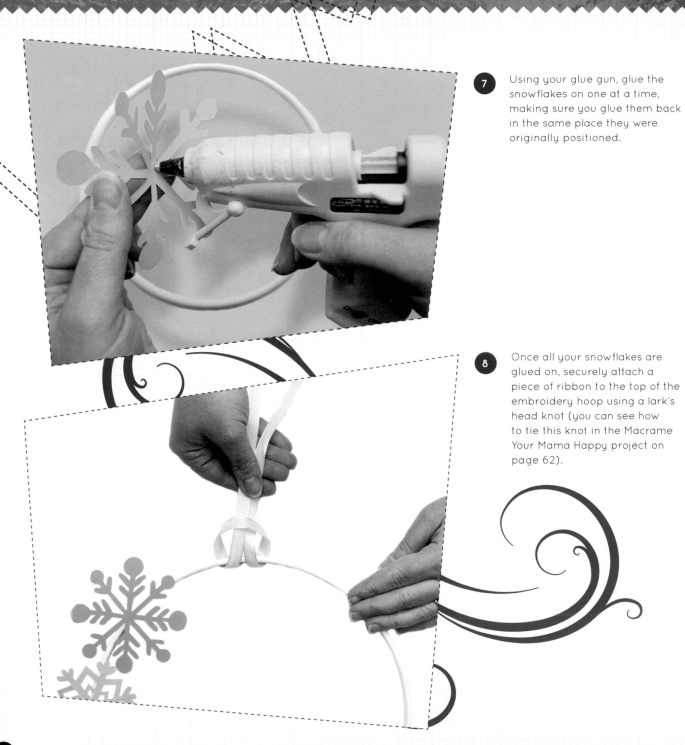

7. Using your glue gun, glue the snowflakes on one at a time, making sure you glue them back in the same place they were originally positioned.

8. Once all your snowflakes are glued on, securely attach a piece of ribbon to the top of the embroidery hoop using a lark's head knot (you can see how to tie this knot in the Macrame Your Mama Happy project on page 62).

YOUR EXTRA TIME AND YOUR *Stitch*

YOU WILL NEED:

- Embroidery hoop
- 18-count cross-stitch fabric (we used Aida)
- Embroidery thread (we used different shades of purple)
- Cross-stitch needles
- Embroidery scissors
- Cross-stitch pattern printed on paper (see page 89)

Stitch your own sassy catchphrase!

Prince had a knack for incredibly memorable lyrics. Always a little odd, and often a little transgressive, his words stick in the mind.

His catchy choruses are more than just an epic hook. His sexy, strident lyrics mix up the mundane, the erotic, and the wildly fantastic to give his songs the tell-tale Prince edge. Even songs written for other bands, such as "Manic Monday" for The Bangles, feature everything from employment levels to the crystal-clear Italian waters of a lover's homeland.

One way to show your admiration for his verbal prowess is to use the craft of cross-stitching. Take inspiration from Prince and get stitching on a bold slogan.

1 Start by preparing your hoop—loosen the screw at the top and take apart the two pieces.

2 Lay your piece of fabric on top of the inner hoop, then replace the outer hoop and tighten the screw fastening. Make sure the fabric is pulled tight in the hoop—it should be almost like a drum!

3 Separate the embroidery thread—each piece of thread is made of six strands, and you need to separate them into two sections of three strands each.

Do this by slowly pulling the piece of embroidery thread apart, letting it untwist as you do so. Don't rush and pull it apart too quickly, because the thread can bunch up and become knotted.

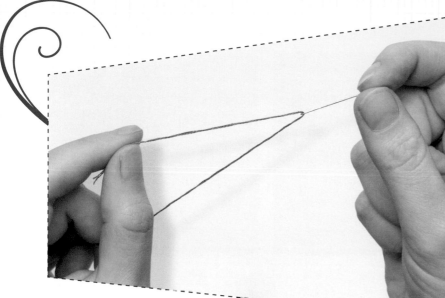

4 Once you have three strands ready, thread your needle with all three strands.

5 You don't need to tie a knot at the end of your thread. Simply push your needle through from the back, in the bottom left of where your first stitch will be, making sure you leave a short tail of thread at the back.

6 Now stitch across diagonally from the bottom left corner to the top right.

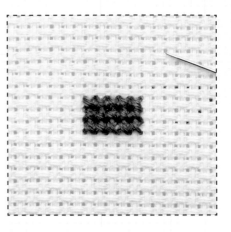

7 Once you've finished this row of stitches, go back and stitch the other half of the X, from the bottom right corner to the top left.

8 Continue across the row, stitching the first half of each stitch type. Keep your tail trapped at the back with each stitch (as shown above).

9 Repeat this process for each stitch, following the pattern to make sure you stitch the correct number of stitches to form the letters. Each black square on the pattern represents one cross stitch.

We recommend marking off each stitch or row of stitches as you work so you don't lose track.

We used a different shade of purple thread for each word, but you can stitch them in any colors you want.

SO TONIGHT I'M GONNA PARTY

Video:

. . . with this sensational wall hanging

Prince had a phenomenal work ethic. By the time he was nineteen, he had produced, arranged, composed, and performed two studio albums.

He went on to create a total of thirty-nine studio albums and four live albums. But that wasn't by any means the end of his creative output. Some of the most successful songs by artists, including Kenny Rogers, Sheena Easton, Sinéad O'Connor, and The Bangles, were penned by Prince, and he was the driving force behind the Minneapolis music scene that emerged in the 1980s. He was forever reaching for the next achievement.

Your mamas would definitely be impressed to see you reviving the 1970s art of macrame. Try these basic knots and create a wall hanging to make somebody proud!

YOU WILL NEED:

- One length of 5 mm cotton cord (we used Bobbiny), about 16 inches (40 cm) long
- 12-inch (30-cm) piece of wooden dowel
- 12 lengths of 5 mm cotton cord (we used Bobbiny), each 5½ yards (5 m) long
- Pair of scissors

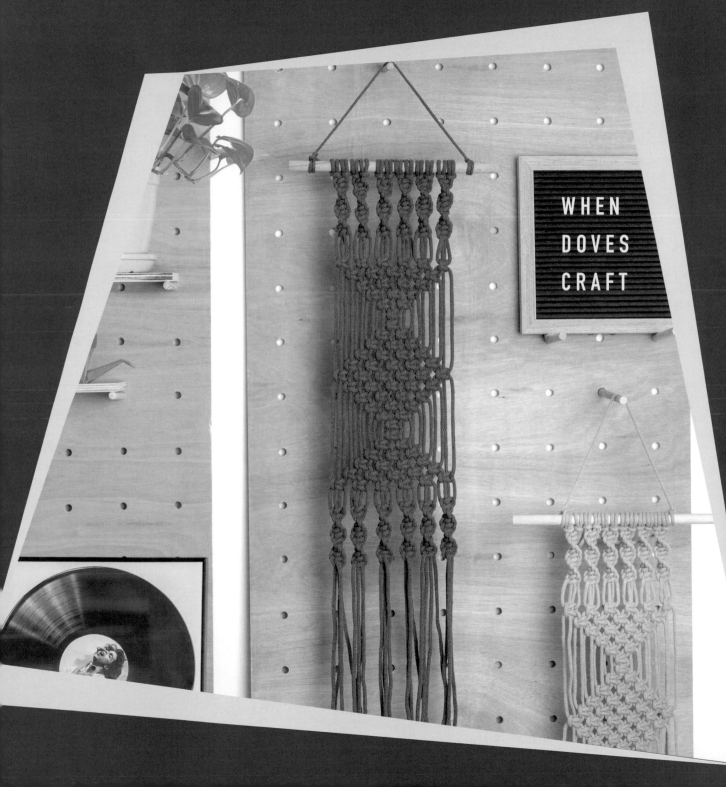

A Knotty Art

It is thought that the macrame technique began in the thirteenth century, when weavers in the Arab world used a system of knots to tie up the loose ends of yarn and thread on textiles that had been loomed by hand. The Moorish conquest brought the art to the West, and it took off with a diverse crowd—everyone from sailors and housewives to the aristocracy.

 Lark's head: step 1
Fold the first 5½-yard (5-m) length of cord in half, then hang it over the dowel, with the folded loop facing away from you.

 Lark's head: step 2
Take the long ends of the folded cord (without the folded loop in it) and thread through the looped part of the cord in a downward direction.

 Setting up the dowel
Beginning with the short piece of cord, tie one end to each end of the wooden dowel. This will allow you to hang it up while you work.

Find somewhere you can stand or sit with the dowel suspended in front of you. We like to stand a dining chair on a table and hang our work from that.

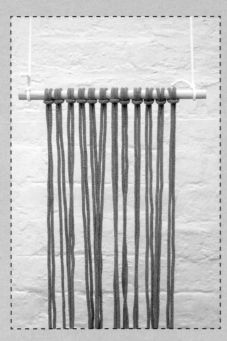

④ Lark's head: step 3

Pull downward on the cord to tighten up and create your lark's head knot. Repeat Lark's Head steps 1–3 with each of your 12 long lengths of cord to create a neat row of lark's head knots. You are now ready to start your wall hanging.

⑤ Spiral: step 1

Start with a row of half knot spirals, which are our personal favorite macrame knot (don't tell the others, we don't want to hurt their feelings). In this project, you will work with two sets of cords at a time, totaling four cords. The middle two cords are your filler cords, and the outer cords are your left working cord and right working cord. Take your left cord and make an L shape with it on top of the other cords. Place the right cord on top of the horizontal part of the L shape.

⑥ Spiral: step 2

Take the right cord behind all the other cords, and bring it out to the front through the gap created by the L between the left cord and the filler cords—make sure you keep hold of the left and right cords.

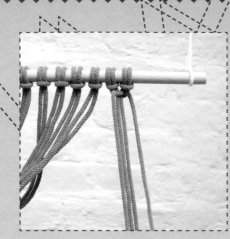

7 **Spiral: step 3**

Tighten the knot by holding the filler cords still and pulling the left and right cords in an upward motion until it reaches the top. This is your first half knot spiral!

8 **Spiral: step 4**

Staying on the same set of four cords, repeat Spiral steps 1–3 to tie another 12 half knot spirals.

9 **Spiral: step 5**

Once you have tied a few half knot spirals it will start to spiral. Don't worry about straightening it out each time—just let it spin. Whichever cord ends up on the left will become your left working cord, because this knot is reversible. To count how many knots you have tied, count the horizontal bars running across the middle of the spiral.

Once you have completed your first spiral, take the next set of four cords and tie another 12 half knot spirals. Repeat with each set of four cords until you have six beautiful spirals.

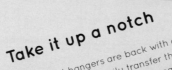

Take it up a notch

Macrame plant hangers are back with a vengeance—you can easily transfer the skills picked up in this project to create your own hangers. Although macrame looks difficult, there are only a handful of different knots to learn. Once you've nailed them, you can create plant hangers galore and give your home a groovy 1970s vibe.

10 **Square: step 1**
You are now going to learn to tie a square knot, which is made in two halves. The good news is the first half of a square knot is identical to a half knot spiral, which you have already mastered! So take your first set of four cords (the ones you tied your first half knot spiral with) and repeat Spiral steps 1–3, but don't tighten the knot all the way up to your spiral. Leave a gap of about 2 inches (5 cm).

11 **Square: step 2**
Once you have tied the first half of your square knot , you are ready to make the second half, which is the reverse of what you have just done. Start by making a back to front L shape with the right cord across the two cords in the center, then bring the left cord over on top of the horizontal part of the L shape.

12 **Square: step 3**
Take the left cord behind all the cords, and bring it out through the gap created by the backward L of the right cord. Tighten up in the same way as for the spiral knot, holding the filler cords still and pulling the left and right cords in an upward motion. Don't pull too tightly, because this may distort your knot. Congratulations, you've now tied a square knot!

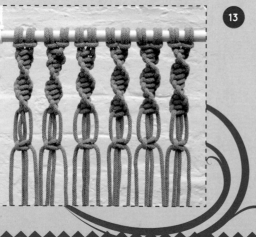

13 **Square: row 1**
Repeat this process with each set of four cords, tying one square knot with each group of cords. The trick to making your work look neat and professional is to make sure each square knot is in line with the previous one, and that the gap between each spiral and square knot is identical.

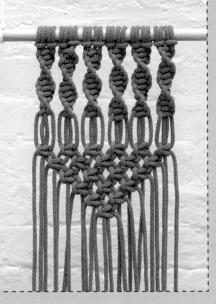

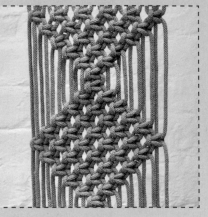

14 **Square: row 2**

You will be making a triangle shape with the square knots. Once you have completed the first row of square knots (there should be six of them), tuck the two cords on the left of your work and the two cords on the right of your work over your dowel, so they are out of the way. You won't need them for the next row. Tie a square knot in what is now the first four cords. This square knot should sit directly beneath and between the first two square knots on the row above.

15 **Square: rows 3–6**

Repeat with each group of four cords until you have five square knots in the row. Continue this process for another four rows, each time tucking away two cords from the left and two from the right. This should mean that you tie one less square knot for each row until you tie only one knot for the final. You should now have an upside-down triangle.

16 **Triangles**

To make a regular triangle underneath, start by tying another single square knot directly underneath your last single square knot. Then bring in two cords from the left and two cords from the right, and use these to tie another row of square knots (there should be two knots in this row.) Then bring in another two cords from each side and repeat the process, so each time you should be tying one more knot for each row until you tie six knots for the final row. Follow this with a row of five knots, then four, three, two, and one, so you end up with a square diamond shape.

17 **Finishing**

To complete your wall hanging, tie a regular triangle underneath your diamond and finish with a final set of half knot spirals. All that's left now is to trim the ends of your work to the length you want and then find somewhere to hang your wall hanging.

Whittle RED CROCHET HOOK

Woodwork a love that's gonna last

Prince wasn't one to shy away from sex in his lyrics, and perhaps the reason some of his early songs were not hits was because they were so explicitly erotic.

But sexuality was at the core of his being, so it's fitting that his first Top-10 U.S. hit was all about a one-night stand.

"Little Red Corvette" on first listen, sounds like a song about a car—but it is all about the briefest of romances. It is full of innuendo, but the meaning was veiled just enough to get the song the radio play it deserved, with nothing too overtly naughty in its joyful, sing-a-long chorus. By 2001, the song was so well loved that Chevrolet was happy to associate with it, putting up a series of billboards reading, "They don't write songs about Volvos." When trying to whittle this racy red crochet hook, aim for a sleek and smooth silhouette—just like the Corvette that inspired it.

Did you know?

Shortly after Prince passed away, Chevrolet tweeted, "Baby, that was much too fast."

YOU WILL NEED:

- A piece of wood about the size of a crochet hook (you can look for a nice twig or branch that's straight); the size you choose depends on the size of hook you want to make
- Hand saw
- Whittling knife
- Red paint suitable for wood (acrylic paint or a nontoxic gloss paint)
- Sandpaper (1 coarse sheet, 1 fine sheet)

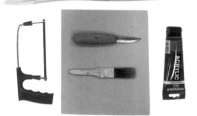

1 Use a saw to cut your wood or twig to a length that fits comfortably in your hand.

2 Hold the wood in one hand, pointing away from you and downward. Push the whittling knife downward and away, along the surface of the wood, so it peels off a top layer. Make sure your hands are behind the knife, out of harm's way.

Dream lover

The lyrics to "Little Red Corvette" came to Prince in a dream, when he was napping in the back seat of singer Lisa Coleman's car.

3 Keep peeling off layers until you have a fairly smooth stick.

4 To form the slightly pointed tip of the hook, use the knife to round off one end of the wood.

5 To form the underside of the hook, push the knife down into the wood at an angle. Then scrape away more wood below the hook, stopping where you meet the cut.

6 Keep cutting and scraping until you have formed a rough hook shape.

 Use sandpaper to sand the surface of the wood until completely smooth.

8 Finally, paint the handle of the crochet hook red and let dry. It's now ready to use!

Templates

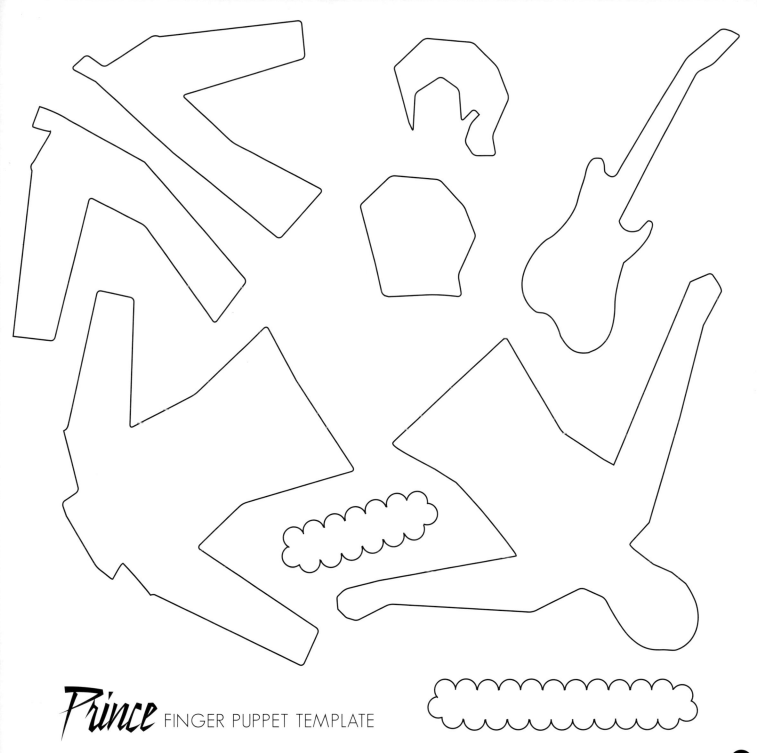

Prince FINGER PUPPET TEMPLATE

I WOULD *Dye* FOR YOU TEMPLATE

YOU GOT THE

Scrapbook TEMPLATE

83

NO PARTICULAR Sign TEMPLATE

Snow IN APRIL
TEMPLATE

SO TONIGHT I'M GONNA PARTY

YOUR EXTRA TIME
AND YOUR *Stitch* TEMPLATE

89

7 June 1958

Prince Rogers Nelson is born in Minneapolis, Minnesota, to a jazz singer mother and musician father

October 1979

His second album, *Prince*, is released, and certified Platinum

May 1983

"Little Red Corvette" goes to no. 6 in the charts, and the video is one of the first by a black artist to feature in regular rotation on MTV

July 1984

The movie *Purple Rain* is released one week before the album of the same name, which sold 13 million copies in the US alone

April 1978

Prince's debut album, *For You*, is released and charts at no. 163

October 1982

1999 sells over 5 million copies worldwide, cementing the Purple One's status as a megastar

July 1994

Prince tops the charts for the first time with "When Doves Cry"

March 1985

He wins the Best Original Score Academy Award for the *Purple Rain* soundtrack

Timeline

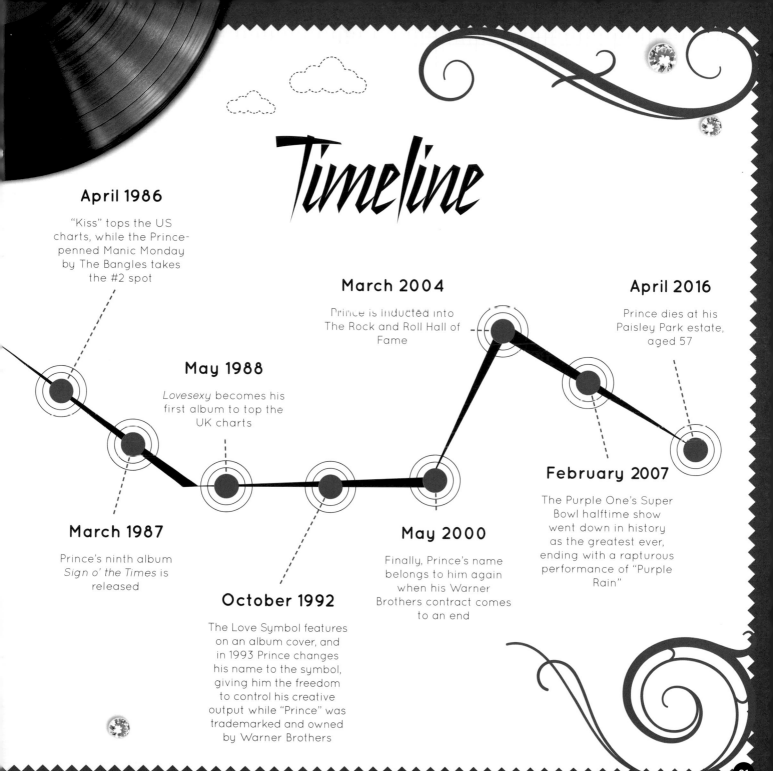

April 1986

"Kiss" tops the US charts, while the Prince-penned Manic Monday by The Bangles takes the #2 spot

March 2004

Prince is inducted into The Rock and Roll Hall of Fame

April 2016

Prince dies at his Paisley Park estate, aged 57

May 1988

Lovesexy becomes his first album to top the UK charts

March 1987

Prince's ninth album *Sign o' the Times* is released

May 2000

Finally, Prince's name belongs to him again when his Warner Brothers contract comes to an end

February 2007

The Purple One's Super Bowl halftime show went down in history as the greatest ever, ending with a rapturous performance of "Purple Rain"

October 1992

The Love Symbol features on an album cover, and in 1993 Prince changes his name to the symbol, giving him the freedom to control his creative output while "Prince" was trademarked and owned by Warner Brothers

WHEN
DOVES
CRAFT

KISS

SO TONIGHT
I'M GONNA
PARTY

Index

WHEN
DOVES
CRAFT

Credits

All photographs © Carlton Books unless stated below. The publishers would like to thank the following sources for their kind permission to reproduce the pictures in this book.

Getty Images: Richard E. Aaron/Redferns 26; /Kristian Dowling/Getty Images for Lotusflow3r.com 14; /Bertrand Guay/AFP 11; /Mick Hutson/Redferns 50; /The LIFE Picture Collection 44, 56, 70; /Frank Micelotta 32, 76, 96; /Tim Mosenfelder 62, 90; /Paul Natkin/WireImage 20; /Christopher Polk/Getty Images for Clear Channel 38

Background textures courtesy of Shutterstock

Every effort has been made to acknowledge correctly and contact the source and/or copyright holder of each picture and Carlton Publishing Group apologises for any unintentional errors or omissions, which will be corrected in future editions of this book.

INSIGHT EDITIONS

PO Box 3088
San Rafael, CA 94912
www.insighteditions.com

Find us on Facebook:
www.facebook.com/InsightEditions
Follow us on Twitter: @insighteditions

Library of Congress Cataloging-in-Publication Data available.

ISBN: 978-1-68383-863-0

REPLANTED PAPER

Insight Editions, in association with Roots of Peace, will plant two trees for each tree used in the manufacturing of this book. Roots of Peace is an internationally renowned humanitarian organization dedicated to eradicating land mines worldwide and converting war-torn lands into productive farms and wildlife habitats. Roots of Peace will plant two million fruit and nut trees in Afghanistan and provide farmers there with the skills and support necessary for sustainable land use.

Manufactured in China by Insight Editions

10 9 8 7 6 5 4 3 2 1